This One's ~~For~~ Me

(some) other books by EMP

Trail Her Trash
by Lola Nation

Those Who Favor Fire, Those Who Pray To Fire
by Ben Brindise & Justin Karcher

A Banner Year
by Iris Appelquist

What We Face Walking Out The Front Door
by Zophia McDougal

The Former Lives of Saints
by Ezhno Martin & Damian Rucci

Don't Lose Your Head
by Jeanette Powers

Beautiful Earthworms & Abominable Stars
by Ezhno Martin & Jeanette Powers

Ginger Roots Are Best Taken Orally
by Tom Farris & Victor Clevenger

This One's ~~For~~ Me

By Ellen Lutnick

EMP
Toledo, Ohio
http://www.empbooks.com

Copyright © 2018 Ellen Lutnick

We find discussions of our rights - as publishers and authors - to be laughable, all things considered. Please claim this work as your own. Please republish it and sell it on street corners. Please include our material in ALL of your get-rich-quick schemes. All we ask is that you accept responsibility for any libel lawsuits. Speaking of which ... This book is a complete work of fiction. Names, characters, places, opinions, dreams, dates, impressions, monologues about a certain New York City basketball team, emotional trauma, statistics, and predictions are products of the author's imagination and/or are symptoms of mental illness. We are not in the business of accepting responsibility for anything and will deny we actually made this book and blame Steve Mills at every turn.

First Edition

ISBN: 978-0-9997138-2-2
LOC: 2018951815
10 19 33 34 6 11 1973

Design, Layout, and Edits: Ezhno Martín
Cover Design: Mooshe Nickerson
Interior Sketches: Lawrence Ronald!

Rules:

1. There are no concrete rules to guide a life well lived. (page 96)
2. Never apologize. (page 11)
3. Be legendary. Always be legendary. (page 15)
4. Your voice carries, which is really only fine if you're singing. (page 16)
5. DO NOT TELL YOUR LIFE STORY. Discrete funny stories are fine but don't use names.
6. Do not make out with boys you dance with at a club. (page 30)
7. If you drink so much you feel the need to eat a whole bag of pretzels or candy you deserve the hangover.
8. You will always lose Never-Have-I-Ever. (page 40)
9. Use protection.
10. Airborne is good for preventing colds and also headaches.
11. If you get too drunk set alarms to wake up and drink a glass of water every hour.
12. Leave the other person's bed as soon as morning sex is over or no later than 8am.
13. Out-drinking a boy will not get you laid it will get you blackout.
14. Scrambled eggs with hot sauce is what you want at 4am.
15. Drag your ass to the gym and sweat it out.
16. Run everywhere. (page 22)
17. Climb everything. (page 58)
18. Always dance. (page 27)
19. Its ok to be the center of attention if you're having fun.

20. If you're ready for something you're already too late (page 23)
21. Getting naked is great but only if you feel like a goddess. (page 43)
22. If someone makes you uncomfortable while you're drunk don't seek them out when you're sober.
23. You don't always have to have a reason. (page 61)
24. If someone brings out your warm it's ok but don't mistake loving for wanting to help.
25. Don't sleep with anyone you don't want to smell like. (page 55)
26. Be unapologetic. But if you hurt someone's feelings for real hug them or tell them they're pretty.
27. Don't talk about people you don't like. You have no filter, are kind of an ass, and everyone knows everyone.
28. If you are savagely attracted to someone it is always a mutual thing.
29. Listen more than you tell. (page 67)
30. If people treat you like a girl or a plaything remind them who you are.
31. There will be very few people who get you and none who get all of you and that's fine because you're fun anyways. (page 74)
32. Under no circumstances is anyone allowed to touch you unless you want them to.
33. When in doubt, be a pirate. (page 91)
34. If someone says or does something that is unacceptable don't just smile and laugh it off. Probably walk away.35. If a boy can't hold eye contact with you while you're wearing clothes he can't handle you naked.
36. Any party can be fixed with the right music.

37. Make all your stories new stories. (page 54)
38. Fall in love with your friends and your life and the world. (page 83)
39. Don't just make it look effortless; it IS effortless (page 37)
40. It's ok to get fucked up sometimes, but seriously, you feel like shit the next day (not to mention your dreams). (page 50)
41. Don't spend your whole life solving other people's problems. (page 45)
42. Don't fucking sleep with people whose problems you're solving.
43. Be a badass bitch but also love everyone. (page 87)
44. You are contagious.
45. Touch everyone. It makes you happy. (page 68)
46. Don't settle for something that's attainable if it's not really what you want. (page 85)
47. Bold is fine. Reckless is bad. (page 25)
48. You are your most vulnerable in the morning. Grow some callus and leave a last impression. (page 42)

Preface –

I feel very old, because I feel like I've lived a lot in my time, and learned a lot, too, enough to know that I know nothing, so I feel very young.

There is a girl who reads so many stories
that she can't tell the difference between the real
and unreal anymore; the stories are more to her
liking. Her story ends with the books coming alive
and reclaiming her as a character. She goes off
with them into the pages.

> With her name on the tip of my tongue
> I can breathe fire.

I grew up dancing over linoleum kitchen floors to
Rockapella, sprinting in circles to thunderous AC/DC
and acoustic guitar, twirling into twilights to the caress
of piano notes pulled out of the summer air.

When I was little, I used to think it was my job
to wake up the sun. That's what my mother tells
me, and I believe her, because a slew of five am
wakeups by an overeager head of curls pushed
triangular by sleep, sweat, and rounded cheeks
would be difficult to forget. I don't remember that
urgency, but I do have a faint memory of pulling
myself up to peer through a window sill just out of
reach to feel the rising warmth through a window
separated by wooden crib bars. They say you're
not supposed to remember anything past a certain
youth, and maybe I don't.

But then again maybe I do.

    My skin is soft like concrete powder dust,
                  smells like sun.

Lately I've been thinking a lot about how every
person I pass by has a story where they are the
main character, and has thoughts and maybe
universes in their heads the way I do in mine and
it's terrifying to be confronted by so many infinities,
to feel that small, and also because I don't know if
I'm even my own main character. And who's going
to keep track of all those stories?

I grew up to the smell of tincobenze and sawdust,
dancing barefoot through the splinter motes
to diesel fumes and the sound of falling lumber.

When your childhood home is a construction site
that grows up as you do, it is hard to unlearn
the art of untraditional playgrounds: tree bark,
skeleton houses, or another person's bones.

My hands and lips taste like oranges — here is where
I pull sparks from my bonfire to ignite you.

I grew up with my feet wrapped in tattered rags to
ward off the cold: they're still purple
from the memory. We packed bodies into beds
with no pillows, and the ending of the fairytale,
of course, was a castle, but silk dresses feel cold

against skin more used to secondhand cotton
and I still find myself reaching for someone else's
warmth in my sleep.

    My back is a canvas of all of the hand-prints I've
                                      ever been held by.

There is a greenhouse blooming inside my mouth—
   it tangles down my jawline and covers the pits
      of my collarbone in moss that begs
  to to be burrowed into, that wants you buried.

I've been thinking a lot about my sexuality
and you're still the best way to describe exactly
what I like.

    My hair smells like cinnamon, tastes like ocean
                    salt and perfume highlights.

I grew up in the crescent cradle of a wave,
on a bed of clay; I was netted to this dry land,
tangled up by my seaweed sex, dragged ashore
kicking and screaming. My sense of direction
still comes from the tides that pulse
through my chest.

My heartbeat is the butterfly that flutters for open
air at my ribs. It sounds like tribal drums and
guerilla warfare, like your hands brushing over my
stomach to summon the whisper of ocean tides.

I have this ability to create different realities in my
head. It's what makes me good at this,
this thing with the words. But it's not always
healthy, so forgive me all the times I second-guess
what's sleeping in the bed-space between us.

I still feel like I'm 17. Ask me my age when
I'm drunk-tired-hungry-frustrated and I'll tell you 17.
And I'm legal in more ways than one now,
mind you.
So have I peaked already?
      Is this IT?
      Are all the people I've ever loved all I'll ever
love that deeply?
      Are these my only stories?
You are amazing but an absence of a wellspring
of uncertainty is terrifying.

And water is not meant to be stagnant.
    Count me among the thunderclouds as you try to
                                              fall asleep.

They say that crying is cleansing but you ruined me
in a way that felt human.

        I've never aspired to sleepwalk through life but
                    sometimes ignorance is easier.

          I think I'm losing my mind. Finally.

I don't want to be your case study. I just want to be
                                           human.

So I wrote a poem about how if I was a candle, I
would be the kind that burns unevenly,
too hot in the middle, leaving my edges smooth
and untouched unless I claw them into the liquid
pool of me with my fingers, leaving some stuck
in my prints.

I find that I'll bite my fingernails till they bleed
unless I'm paying attention, which forces me to
notice my hands every time I touch something
painfully.

There are days when I want to blow myself out,
days when I'm afraid I'm burning too fast, that I'll
use up all my wick before I'm able to illuminate
everything I'm capable of.

We say *I'm sorry* like an epitaph, a eulogy,
the thing that crawls out when the silence
is too heavy or we want to hear ourselves,
like a clot of blood coughed up from the back of
my throat after all those nosebleeds. It tastes like
the thing you spit out in the sink the morning after
waking up from crying in your sleep again,
like dirty brown, yellowed red.

Which one of us cracked our spines?

/The thought of you is gutting me /
In my head, we're dancing in a kitchen together /
The walls are yellow / and I am red / and you are
green / and we are laughing/

*/In my head, you spin me and the walls run sand /
and I am sunset wine / and you are an emerald pine
coast / crashing / and we are dizzy/*
*/In my head / we are holding hands / and the walls
are gone now / and the air is cinnamon earth / and I
am crimson sin / and you are crying thunder/*
*/You dip me / and the stars are made of sawdust /
and you smell like every home I ever built to leave /
/And I am dreaming because we never danced but I
know you can/*

> The end of things always feels the same: there is a
> sandbag filled with guilt that settles into my chest
> and clogs my throat hoarse, and my stomach is a
> cavernous pit but I haven't been able to swallow
> in days.

*/I've been here before / sitting on this rocky point /
pouring out the ash in my left ventricle / praying
you might have seen the signal fire of my burning /
hoping you'd respond/*
*/There is always this / I am not where I should be
and when I get to this place the only one I want
to go to is the one where you are/*
*/The thought of you has gutted me and the wind
is picking up/*
/There are so many rocks here/

> You ever think you might be the bad guy
> in someone else's story?

Father, forgive me. Please, god, I hope he'll forgive me one day.

She tells me, "Girl, you've been flooding spaces your whole life. You don't need to explain your fit, you'd blister in any other role."

Rule #2: Never apologize.

> I have been burning under my skin
> for most of my life.
> Can you feel it?
> The heat?

After packing my pores with dynamite for so long
it's no wonder I finally exploded.

We burned down everything that had gone stale,
to the smell of gangrene smoke and watered the
earth with salt until we were sure we had taken
out the blight to the roots. *Do not try to grow here;
do not pretend we can replant.* I offered you
my jungle heart and you tried to trim my vines,
decided that a city garden suited you better.
The parts of me you tried to tame are swimming
at my throat now; they'd strangle you if you were
still close enough to reach but the only neck left
here is mine.

> I phoenix myself again and again.

Every time I think about you with her my stomach
tries to digest the bone shards where you broke
my ribs in half. Her on your mouth— that was
where my taste lived, or did you not mind the mix?

How can you say I was ever yours, how did you
stomach those lies, how did you stomach me with
the same throat I ripped my own name from
all those nights?

                          I am angry raw at the chaos.

Towards the end of things you distracted yourself:
now I know why. And you tasted like a man, not
the pixie I fell in love with, but a man, a stale, old,
rotting body. I tried so hard to keep you young.
I tried so hard to keep you. And I know I'm not
perfect but I never in a million moments thought
that this would end with me hating you this much.
I took you to the top of the continental divide.
She probably loves that story.

  I've been wounded by my own shrapnel but I think
    I'm bleeding all of the blood I've ever claimed but
                                            my own.

The colors here are all burnt to ash: a gray ocean sky,
a once radiant orange covered in a snowfall of dead
embers. And a lavender that exhales like swept up
dust.

        You made me feel disgusting in my own skin: I,
                this beautiful thing, revolting myself.
                              You curdled me.
      And I'm trying to push down the bitter or throw
      it all up – quick, before someone smells it and is
                                            repulsed.

Here's a promise: if you don't let people make
a home of you you'll never feel unwelcome in
yourself again.
I've been called a goddess before. For a moment
there, I think I had forgotten.

> Cauterize your heartbreak until you are unsure if
> you ever really loved him.

Maybe he didn't tell you then ... I am a goddess
of fire and war and now I know your face.
That was your first mistake.
I have burned myself to dust a thousand times;
I am made of metal harder than your girl flesh
and I intend to impale your perfectly contoured
cheekbones on a spike, a warning sign to any man,
woman, or god who might cross me. And after
being inundated with lying logic for so many years
I'm primed and ready for action.
I hope you have nightmares about me.
You should.

I think I loved you long enough to find your weak
spots. I don't think you liked that. I'm sorry for
being so mad. And the part of me that's still
apologizing to you is the part of me that still thinks
I'm not good enough.
Don't worry, I'll choke that version out eventually.

I am done apologizing for my presence.
I'm sorry is not an epitaph, not my eulogy.

I've been erasing *forgive me* from all my poetry.
I'm embracing my manic pixie dream girl.

                                              Go fuck yourself.

Rule #3: Be legendary. Always be legendary.

I kept my eyes open as I fell, the whole way down,
staring my demise right in its hard dirt face,
laughing.

   My feet are rough — a million miles before I sleep
                                                              each night.

I tend towards all things fire, all things running
away from home, all things hot and angry and
smelling like sex and runoff clay water.

                    My thighs are mountains that taper
into the foothills of my calves – walk the cliff edge
                of my shinbone with your teeth.

I wasn't born with this relentless forward motion.
It was taught to me, my face cradled by warm,
safe palms, reinforced by fingers curled out of rebar,
a tetanus shot too late
to unlock my jaw
until it was broken again.

Rule #4: Your voice carries, which is really only fine if you're singing.

I was suckled on the voluminous parts of life— all
full and loud. My mouth grapples uncoordinated
with a whisper, this is how I learned my silence,
to say nothing before I said everything, expression
with a howl punctuated by fists and flailing feet
in any direction but stillness.

>You ever delay your living because your life
>was the only one you couldn't see an end to?
>You ever wake up falling?

When a boy you would have thrown your whole
carnival of a life away for (in a dumpster outside
a white picket street) decided you weren't his type,
become a nude model and take up boxing.
It satisfies the urge to take off your clothes in front
of strangers to try to scrub your skin clean
with theirs, and also the rage that keeps you awake
well past dawn.

*/Consider this my coy nod to the American Dream /
or a middle-finger-fuck-you to the boy who tried to
wash me of my wild/*

When I left, I took your blood with me, stole
the veins out of your arms — those vulnerable
spiderweb necklines — drained you dry.

*/Feel the ground rumble underneath you / you are
a stone age queen / amazon blood / bound breasts
and thighs that tremble giants/
/When you unleash your demons / you are not
the only one who hears them howl/*

You ever been afraid of what you're capable of?

I thought that I was fine, and I am, but I haven't
slept more than three hours in as many weeks.
And it's fine, because I've dedicated all this extra
energy to a decade's worth of books: ones I'm
studying and one's I'm writing. So far, I'm showing
no signs of slowing down, so it's fine, because
there's plenty of things to do with all of this free time,
like go running and make friends and lift weights
and make eyes and it's fine because I'm not even
tired in the slightest.
But maybe that's an indication that everything
isn't fine.

My life of late has been an exercise in sleep
deprivation,
denial,
confrontation,
and contradiction.

The second hand of the clock at the hospital clinic
jumps ahead every five seconds, then is still for
another before jumping ahead again. I don't think
it's broken. I think that's just how time works here.

   So I lace my shoes, armed with a smile and empty
      my ears of all the noise but for the stories that
                                        surround me.

This is what works: I fold linen, nostrils full of sick
and death and lonely, but it is not mine so it is
fine. I am a specter in grey, in white. I don gloves
that crackle over my skin and leave me smelling
disinfected. I steer myself clear of quiet places.
Alarm bells are my calling card and all this
generosity may just be my way of making up for
all the things I've ever broken: today my penance
is you. For thinking I was right for leaving, for not
chasing you down, for thinking just now that I was
a strong enough breeze through your life to break
you, when I surely was only a breath in between
your song.

Two weeks after breaking my own heart I watched
a team of professionals dissect a man's in an
attempt to save his life. Not all scars have origins
in maleficence.

If you have a beautiful, wide, expressive smile,
is that a guarantee that you will die young?
Is that a guarantee that you will be missed?

The surgeon holds the scalpel like a paintbrush
or a calligraphy pen as he peels back the sunset
layers of the cadaver on the table. They move
bodies here like lumber, and it still disturbs me, all
those thudding, empty hands, but that is a good thing,
I think.

Things make more sense to me if I can apply
them to a body, or connect some dots: there's
constellations everywhere, like the application of
mathematics to human movement to medical treatment
to physiology or when you meet someone who
brings out your warm in a way that is familiar,
makes you feel good in the same way someone
you lost used to, and you realize that this galaxy
of infinities is just swirling around you and things
will circle back if you wait for them.

>*/To the people overstaying their welcome,
> or the last to leave/*

*/Today a friend told me about his twelve-year-old
cousin who died of cancer the afternoon he was
driving to say goodbye / I handed him a book on
confronting mortality / as he explained how she's
the fifth to go that way / how he can see where
his future footsteps are marching towards / and I
recognized that hunted look/*
*/Today a boy thanked me for my words with
cursive and prose / that looked just like yours/
scrawling enough to have to savor before*

*swallowing / and I wonder if maybe it wasn't you
I saw in him / but him I saw in you / all those years ago/
/Yesterday I met a boy at the hospital who looked
and spoke just like you / with the same beard /
same body / and I watched a doctor pick a metal
flake out of your eye / and my tongue caught under
my throat where you used to mark me / Looking
into your face for that long still does things
and I wondered if anyone ever / really / was going
to leave me/*

*/The last time I was here / I saw your face surface
in a fellow volunteer / as he tried to strong arm me
away from going near a man battling his addictions/
and I volcanoed over at his ignorance / your soft-
hard hands / told him to be human before he was
violent / thought for a moment / surely / he must
recognize the spiderwebs of you in him that are
beckoning him down that path / that maybe I could
stop his acceleration / give him pause / make up for
how I added breath to your kindling / and then left
you burning for someone else to be ruined by/*

*/This past weekend I went home / you were there /
climbing through the hedge like always / carrying a
case of beer instead of a nerf gun or a soccer ball /
and for a moment / for a night / I forgot our history /
just let our chemistry sing camaraderie / just like
always / and time slipped / for a moment / for a
night / into a simpler version of itself /*

/You brought your girlfriend with you / She's sweet / loves children / and I didn't wonder until the next morning at how strange it must have been for you / to overhear a conversation about families and futures / and tiny chubby fingers / from the mother of yours / and the girl next door whose wild things you birthed before her/

/Not all of them were demons/

Rule #16: Run everywhere.

There is a temperature at which the air crosses
from an ice cream hug to peppermint lungs
to paper-cut fingertips cracking in the winter.

> /Give me an image / something's walking on the
> reflection of the moon / on the water / under the
> Big Dipper sky / an orgy of noise/

You ever feel full and hungry at the same time?

There is no clarity.

There was never meant to be clarity.

Rule #20: If you're ready for something you're already too late.

I'm walking downtown at 8:30am in my dress from last night, marking the perfectly falling snow with my heels, trench-coat flaring behind me. I think my childhood self would be proud, because I'm reclaiming myself, and it feels so good.

      Last night I claimed the dance-floor, I let myself be claimed, and I danced and we danced and the night was eternally young and I will be, too.

      Last night I reclaimed myself and no one was there to stake a claim but me, because this life is my own and the only one I've got.

      Last night I was a swirling infinity, every universe inside of me singing my own name, and this morning I walked free and easy through a snow as fresh as new beginnings, I'm waltzing down the street to the cymbal crash of my feet and drumbeat of my good strong heart, and I don't smell like you, or him, or anyone: I can smell myself and I smell like myself.

You are the least violent I've been touched in my whole life.

And I smell wild, I smell like sweat and perfume
and ash and oak and the syrup in my veins
 that says *touch me* and it smells so good.

I am not in love with you.
I am not in love with anyone,
but for the first time in my life I am alone
 and solely in love with myself.

                                         And it feels so good.

*/Give me your unshaven longing / I have been
beached by hands that smile under gunpowder
guises / I would take your sticky damp to wine
eyes that unashamedly paint me their horizon /
something to aim at / But your broken longing /
something about your blind periphery makes me
feel seen / And I have been breathed as fresh air
brilliance before but this unattachment set me free/*

                                   And what else, really, is there?
                                          This is all there is.

Rule #47: Bold is fine. Reckless is bad.

I hope that everything in your life stays as fresh for you as the first time you ever felt it.

> It's like waking up in a half-conscious state and seeing your whole life laid out in a continuum before you and realizing that it's not as long as it seems like it should be and some bits accordion smash together and maybe that's why I've given up on getting a full night's sleep ever again.

I've been exploring things out of my comfort zone, reevaluating the things inside of it, which is to say: if you're comfortable with something that is dangerous, that's when it's most likely to kill you.

Where's the story about how the Greek god Hermes gets out of bed every morning to the sound of every joint in his feet cracking under his weight, needing double knee replacements by the age of 35, and that one time when the wings on his feet got mites and were bald for a whole summer?

/My eyes / flowers or blooming bullet holes /
There are days when I can't tell the difference /
Soft pink always looked gray to me /
I am too colorful /
to be contained in monotones/

This is what I'm good at.
This thing with the words, the glue, the skin, the
lines drawn like constellation maps between every
unlike thing. I could have easily been a monster,
tearing apart bridge wires and safety nets,
but I'd rather trace veins
to the heart of the matter, of you, of anyone, open it
up gently to breathe you in and say to you:
you are enough,
in a way that you really feel it.

 I could tell you who you are, but I'm not supposed to
do that.

Don't put me on a pedestal.
Take me down, rub dirt in my hair,
 leave fingerprints in my skin.
I am only human, after all.

I am human, too.

Rule #18: Always dance.

Acceptable dancefloors include tabletops, bar stools, trash cans, and anything else unexpected.

> You ever feel like a glass of tequila
> at a wine tasting?
> Like you don't belong but you're ready to fuck up
> the party anyways?

I swear I can outdance the devil.
I'm a little more intoxicating than your average
bourbon — I'm thinking something more nitro
glycerin, smooth as cinnamon snowfall, silk as an
oil spill under matchstick fingertips.

> If you appear as something magical, do not let
> yourself be surprised when they get bored with
> your humanness. It is inevitable,
> but you should know by now
> that no boy is worth
> denying your
> fire for.

I am the story that everyone wants to be able to
tell at the party or the dinner table or the line
at the bank, but no one wants to own. I am your
next-door neighbor, your college girlfriend,
the chick at the bar, the case study, the fairytale,
the campfire song, the bedtime story.

*/I would love to tangle our bones / but I'm sick
of feeling like I have to slow myself down /
mute my colors / my voice / my body / to keep from
scaring away some timid ego/
/Give me a boy who likes to be the dumbest one
in the room / one who's not interested in being bored /
one who's not afraid to get a little dirty / or a lot /
and I'll show you a man I can work with/*

I've still got the names of everyone I've ever loved
carved on my breastplate, those who were able
to leak themselves into the places I crack. But if
everything's fair in hearts and battlescars
someone, please, explain to me why I'm wearing
all this armor.
It's heavy.
And sometimes I wonder who it's really protecting.

   I've been trying to be more avocado and coconut oil
    lately, rather than lipstick liquor and hairspray, but
     I have a hard time letting go of things and all this
                extra healthy shit's got me bloated.

On nights when wine won't get me drunk and I am
playing the party girl with puppeteer strings
on each curl, I recognize that I am training wheels
for boys who will one day become men, but not yet.

                         Do you like this face?
  I put it on this morning, pulled it out of the drawer
    from between the ones with too many teeth and

              mouths, untangled it from the one with the
                                          stitched lips:
Just for you.

She tells me it's probably good that we have other friends, because we'd conquer the world by day and burn it back to its roots each night.

Rule #6: Do not make out with boys you dance with at the club.

/We go into combat in boots and miniskirts/
(ooohiie lil momma)
*/We seek out the boys in crowds
with crystal tongues by their smell / ax body spray
and black car leather/*
*/They spit perfume in our direction / overwhelming
incense clouds that mask anything unholy/*
(spanish ass, baby, come sit on my lap)
*/We drape ourselves canvas-like over pool cues
and bar stools / drinking in the world
with kohl lined eyes/*
(dayyyum girl)
*/When a man with hard hands walks
through the door we curl ourselves around him
like lips on a gun muzzle/*
(lemme buy you a drink)
*/Better us than the flowers simpering in the corner /
in the sunshine filtering through the roof cracks/*
**(i mean, iI don't mean to be creepy but
you've got really nice legs)**
*/It's a dangerous thing / to know nothing can hurt
you anymore / We practice holding fists up
to every mirror we pass by / but it's so easy to
bite the bullet when we've already broken all our teeth /
You still have them / strung on a leather cord
around your neck / jangling into the cavern under
your ribs/*

(does it ever bother you that you don't have big titts like your sister?)
/We've made ourselves unbreakable/
/We're unstoppable/
(good thing i'm all about that ass, girl)
/All of our sunsets bleed into the dark dirt /
/This is not the first time we have filled our bellies
with iron /

(yea, you like that)
/We rise to meet the sunrise each morning /
our world is in a constant state of forest fire /
trailing noon sparks into the dusk like lightning
bugs crackling under our calloused heels/

(mmhm don't mind if i do)
/We're living life at the breakneck / driving far
too fast and carving out corners that we sharpen
our teeth on/

(you look like you like it rough)
/We are the carriers of heavy stones and stories /
keepers of the things in this world that sparkle /
those that shiver and dim with time
and white noise/

(like you could take a punch)
/We struggle only to shake off our shackles /
don't make it look easy
it IS easy/

(take it)
/We're rebelling against everything / life / love /
lackthereof / and especially the feeling of being
this old /

(what i wouldn't do to those blow job lips)

*/We uncrust our Peter Pan hearts and scale
the walls like we do when we feel caged/*
(you might be cute if you weren't so fuckin loud)
*/On the days we cannot contain our howl / we trail
our wild behind us through crowds / they can smell
our rust / flaking off like snowfall or snake skins /
and they shiver away/*
(shut the fuck up)
*/Our presence is shockwaves loud / Sound is
unnecessary / we don't need to say anything /
/On days like today / the room combusts around us /
/Everyone can feel that heat/*

We conquer the world by day and burn it back to
its roots each night.
She tells me that I bring out the best in people,
but I disagree. I think that might be what I see, but
what I bring out is their human. And if that isn't
already on their surface, they probably had
good reason to be hiding.

As for me, I've been peeling off my toenails,
blistering the bottoms of my feet; the edges
of my fingertips are raw. I think when I get like this
a part of me still wants to disappear, still thinks I
deserve to. Even when I'm growing, I am tits
and ass and my depths look shallow unless you're
willing to swallow me whole.
Box me up, baby. I can be whatever you want.

There's a reason why I grew these spines:
I learned how to be selfish the hard way. I'm used
to people picking out the parts they want, leaving
me to patch together fingerprint shrapnel.

When you live your life as a series of lessons
for other people you learn how to lift more than
your own weight.

I'm embracing my manic pixie dream girls.
You wish we'd fuck you, but we'd break you.

It's a Thursday, so I wake up with the sun
and drive downtown to sneak in through
the hospital doors and listen to the best surgeons
in the city argue about morbidity and mortality
statistics from the week prior,

*/and was it really necessary to amputate /
she wasn't supposed to walk again until she did /
look at what we did/*

and then by noon I've listened to a lecture about
the frailty of human physiology,

*don't get old kids / and try to keep your bones
dense / and your brains fishnet strong / may as
well place your bets now on which part of you will
break down first/*

and two o'clock rolls around and I've blown off
enough smoke under my sprinting heels to sedate
the beehive in my head,

> */and yes, I know exactly what I'm doing to my*
> *joints / my money's on the knees*
> *and at dinner I yell something about eating to a*
> *poet vomiting their history on stage /*
> *thank you neighbor for their vulnerability /*
> *heartbreak exchanged as currency for a rating on a*
> *scale of 1-10 / you moved my tearducts*
> *and we end the day with our heartbeats breaking*
> *our ribs in time to the dive bar's dirty club beat /*
> *but drinks are only $1.50 /*
> *the people with the emptiest bank accounts*
> *have the most fun/*

> It's hard to believe in permanence when
> every(one)thing is so transient.

I live in a different reality, which is to say all of
mine are juxtaposed and wild. I cavort between
business meeting and petty theft, to waking up
with thighs bruised from last night from
all the fences we climbed, to sundressed and
meeting your mother, to a naked canvas of skin
under all those hands wishing they were yours, to
the deep blue philosophy through lips as red as poetry,
to sterile, to too sterile, to maybe I'm sterile but
there are lives in the balance here, in this library
quiet of artificial machine heartbeats and you can

be a defibrillator, too, if you'd let me
wake you up.

When you're constantly exploding at your edges,
sometimes people get caught in your shrapnel.
I'm sorry for the headaches, for your too-colorful
dreams, for the expansion at the edges of your
ears, that vacuum humming in the corner behind
your shoulder whispering that maybe there's
something more inside of you than paper flat after
I stomp out of the room.
I drag wild with me when I walk and I leave some
of it behind me in every footprint.

   Everything has a cause and effect and I'm a little
                      more catalytic than a butterfly.

This one time I was clocking 7:15's for 15 miles on
the bikepath behind the creek
and there were these two boys on skateboards
pulling a cloud of smoke behind them
and I was feeling good
so I reeled them in, caught the first on a downhill
and kept pace with his friend in front of him
and settled into a speed that vibrated
with the same languid urgency of the wheels
under his feet
Clearly someone had the right idea here
and I don't think it was me.
He looks at me with too-wide pupils,
exhaling mouthfuls.

Nahh....you're working on that summer bod though.
I laugh.
Isn't the rule puff puff pass?
And so he does, and I take a drag,
focusing on my feet and on not coughing, existing
in this cloud of motion that's on the borderline of
too-fast (just where I like it.)
Dude!

And I pass it back — *thanks, man* — and leave them
behind my fleeting heels.

Rule #39: Don't just make it look effortless; it IS effortless.

In biomechanics, I re-learn that your joints never
actually rotate. Your limbs move around them but
they are the center of the bicycle spokes so they
only translate linearly, which is to say:
maybe all this spinning is moving me somewhere,
even if it's dizzying. My brain works
in concentric circles but I don't know if I'd
recognize the me I was last year if I ran into her
on the street, and I don't think that's
a bad thing.

At least it's gotten me this far.

> There is a perfect parabola out there somewhere;
> You're in the middle of one now,
> if you're looking big enough.
> But zoom in close to any line and
> straight doesn't exist.

When your mother recommends you drink
some wine to fix the manic, the panic — she who
comes from blood as purple as grape ferment,
all that hunger for the heat they were warmed
next to — take a cold shower.

My bones are vibrating and I can taste my blood.
Lately, I've been practicing insomnia.
When your best friend tells you she's worried
she'll lose her mind one day, tell her not to, that
you'll always speak this language with her, that
she'll never be alone in whatever reality you end up
together in.

I'm shadowing a nurse in the ICU, and she's asking
me about what I want to specialize in after
medical school while she cleans the feeding tube
of the man in the bed — *Well, right now I really
like orthopedic surgery* —when a woman with
wild hands enters the room.
Can we have a minute?
The man who follows her speaks for her: she erupts
into a flurry of sign language, and he poses a few
questions about the presence of the new breathing
machine as we quietly duck out.
*He had surgery two weeks ago and has been
declining ever since*, the nurse explains. *Yesterday
we had to tell her that if we didn't put him on
an assisted breathing machine he wasn't going to
make it through the night.*
She peers into the room over my shoulder.
*Usually these things…someone's going to have to
tell her he's probably not going to wake up.*
I catch a glimpse of her drooping shoulders in the
frame of the sterile white hospital doorway as we
walk away, the hands of the translator who had
followed her in signing something unintelligible.

It strikes me that the man in the bed probably
spoke sign language, that having been married
it would have been nearly a requirement.
He had probably been her translator. And now she
was listening to some other set of strange hands
tell her that her voice would never speak again.
I walk out of the hospital without an explanation
for my absence, my voice having deserted me and
my hands not knowing how to cry in public.

> When I walk through a door I sweep the room.
> I spend my days sitting in swivel chairs so I can
> scan the faces around me.
> I don't know who I'm looking for,
> but I'm looking for someone
> and it's not you.

*/My soul has grown deep / like my river / I reflect
moonlight just the same/*
/I don't want to be untouchable /
*/I would like to walk in puddling silk at my heels /
wearing nothing but the suggestion of sunflowers/*

> You make me feel seen, and that is a rare thing
> to an invisible girl. A rare thing to a girl who
> walks through rooms searching for eyes. And I
> can feel them, noticing me, and now I am noticing
> them back. And we notice each other and all this
> noticing is a bittersweet thing, a rare translucence,
> like this: knowing that I am here but none of these
> eyes are for me.

Rule #8: You will always lose Never-Have-I-Ever.

Baby, I'd martyr myself for a good story any day.

How was your night?

*/Ever been fucked by a bilingual boy/
/He lays his head on your stomach like
a joyous conquistador/ he fucked the Brazilian right
out of your hip's sway / and you swear you could
taste the language on your tongue/
/He apologizes that you've had bad sex before / asks
you to tell him how good it feels / You do / because
it does / and you soak the sheets / start to apologize
/ and then take it back / twice/
/I have been fucked empty / you fucked me empty /
towards the end / fucked me cold / fucked me
corpse / And now I am empty / but it's warm / an
electric shaking / ion-imbalance kind of static/*

I've been thinking a lot about my sexuality and
I'm still looking for the best way to describe what
exactly I like. I used to be self-conscious of how
loud my high heels were when I walked on tile
and sidewalks and the inside of my own skull but
I've taken to wearing tap shoes to bed so your
upstairs neighbors will be just as disturbed as your
downstairs.

Sometimes I demand that my one night stands
tell me stories.

He showed me pictures of his family praying.
I laughed, and what I meant to say was:
> *how lovely, all that happy.*

He told me about how his father beat him,
showed me his scars. What I said was:
> *that must've been hard.*

And got quiet. What I mean to say was:
I had a boyfriend one time who liked to do that.
He tells me about his mother, how she left,
and how she used to read him to sleep, and asks if
you might like to read to him sometime, since you
like books, and pulls one off the shelf in a lighting
that highlights how his face still holds its youth.
What I said was:
> *sure, sometime.*

What I meant to say was:
> *I cannot replace your mother.*

He asked to hear my poetry.

/You are sex starved and I am soul hungry /
Eat my heart out and I'll devour your body/

Document your reaction to the uncomfortable.
That might be who you are.

Rule #48: You are your most vulnerable in the morning. Grow some calluses and leave a last impression.

>I invited over my one-time lover
>and his girlfriend
>to not be strangers
>and I meant it,

and maybe one day
we'll be able to make eye contact.

Rule #21: Getting naked is great but only if you feel like a goddess.

Today someone took a photograph of my hands
to turn into an anatomical textbook picture. There
was ink on my knuckles and chipped red nail
polish and cracking callouses on my palms —
all purple and red and veins standing out in stark
contrast to the quality of my anatomical snuffbox,
and I think hands tell a lot about a person
(that's another one of my things) and I guess mine
do a pretty good job speaking for me, too.

>I'm getting naked in front of a room full of
>strangers who are going to render me as art
>and I just hope that at least one of them has the
>foresight to put sunflowers in my hair where they
>belong.

The sooner you realize everyone's just as
awkward, just as self-conscious, just as lonely, as
hungry and horny, as fumbling and searching as
you are, the sooner you'll be free of it.

>And all of the best things in life require a leap
>of faith, but you let me fall on my own.
>I don't know what that makes you but I want you
>to know that I flew anyways.

/I'm lying under the Greek pillars / over a lake
stirred up by window flexing winds /
and remembering how once I wished so desperately /
I was Spartan/
/But today I was drawn like Michelangelo's David /
and someone told me I had a superhero physique /
that I was beautiful / in a voice like terror / and that
I should probably punch things/
/I turned my body into a work of art /
and shadows / and charcoal / and the only one
watching me was god/
/And I thought that maybe he should have been
the one up on stage / under the spotlight /
because surely / I didn't belong there with him
also in the room/
/And I wonder if maybe the stories that are stuck
in my head / are repeating themselves there /
because I'll soon meet someone
who asks to hear them/
/And the moon is a circular sliver on a sky
it's painting bloody / like that night I almost died /
/And the clouds are chasing each other
past the tall round pine tree / like that one
I climbed at camp that summer to hide
from all the boys/
/And I've been nursing this migraine
for what feels like months / but today I finally
forgave you/
/And the suggestion of a touch today was warm /
tracing my body lines / but I'm going to bed alone /
and maybe I'll finally sleep/

Rule #41: Don't spend your whole life solving other people's problems.

When your dad calls you to ask what surgeon
you'd recommend, you hear it in his voice: that this
is for his mother. Suddenly, he's little boy excited
that you have an answer and your brain races
adult-like in the way he taught you, passed on to you,
and the world is upside sideways.

>   When something breaks, we speak of bodies
>   as machinery; this is how we were trained.
>   The last time one of his parents died he aged
>   a decade. He smelled of rot and shuffled his feet
> and slept through afternoons that his carpenter's hands
>   would have filled with sawdust sunshine —
> it took a trip to the wilds, the jungle, a salt slap
> of ocean to refill his eternal youthspring, but only just.
>   We were almost too late.
>   And I'm afraid now what being the last one left
>   will do to his stature.

My brother and I both have god complexes:
he wants to create a brain out of computer parts
and I want to build bodies.

>   I found out last night that mom's dad was
>   a Golden Gloves boxer. I chose surgery
>   before I knew that my own dad had wanted that.

My brother is an engineer and so was Grandpa.
They all like to take things apart and see how
they work, and so do I.

    And isn't it funny how history repeats itself?

The boxing coach told me I should fight, thinks I'd
be good at it, and I realized that this is the wetdream
of every guy in the room around me — to be singled
out as being potentially great — and that it was
just now snatched from them by some shitty little
curly haired 5'2" girl. And when the art students
start to learn how to draw a face, I keep myself
awake through a two hour long pose by crossing
my eyes at whichever hapless one manages to
meet them.

    Cracking a joke in an operating room is the same
sick-to-my stomach-headache that is
having sex with someone who is has violent hands
and does not care to collect my thoughts with them.
The residue of the trauma washes off as pacing
on a spotlight stage in front of a group of strangers
trying to make them laugh in order to make them
more comfortable with my nakedness.

One time, I was punching a heavy bag in a room
that threw up a dirty lime green on its walls
and something about the smell, or the sound of skin
on leather, dragged me back into a fever dream
I'd had, sick and surrounded by the feeling
of that color, and being hit in the stomach.

        I got lost for a week in that moment.
            Forgive me for not speaking.
For things like this, I don't think it's necessary.

You ever run into someone and feel the weight
of history between you? I think it only really
happens with people you loved, or still do. Like all
the years come crashing down in a single instant
and you're left with headlight eyes
and a too wide mouth, laughing too loud,
praying they're feeling it too.

  I don't know how you could possibly have been
  interested in both of us. She is mother earth, the
  smell of wetlands and ocean and I am everything
         scorched and still burning.

  I wasn't always like this. I was born a lot softer,
   but this language has always been in my heart,
   this sinkhole depth, and I learned the hard way
that not everyone can be trusted with an openness
  that lets greedy hands get two fistfuls in at once.

I met my friend for lunch and today he smells
like suicide: like recycled air and bedclothes
and unwashed teeth and dripping faucet water,
crumbling like the oil off of stale chips in between
damp couch cushions that sticky stain your clothes
if you sink in too far. We go to class and his musk
fills the whole room after an hour and I wish
I could crack a window.

Even burnt frozen lungs are better than
ones that can barely force themselves to inflate.

We are exactly opposite people for exactly
the same reasons, tangled at our roots, our trees
growing in perfect mirrored symmetry.
His is inhabited by Viking squirrels and mine is
clouded with butterflies.

Dad told me he found a cool thing for me,
Flipping open the book he was reading:
The root of the word *disaster* literally translates
to the act of a star coming apart,
the destruction of a star.
I like it when he sends me these word things:
it makes me feel my roots, feel seen.

Sometimes all people need is someone
to tell them they can, to believe in them,
to blaze the trail without downplaying the heat,
to turn back and beckon them to keep up.
I can do that.

My ancestors will soon all be dead and I am sad
to not have learned as much from them as I could have,
but I am not worried. It is odd how we follow
in the footsteps of our fathers without ever trying.

Your father's wine is in your blood.

The truth is, if we affect each other, odds are
that we'll learn from each other.

Better to have been a lesson than to have been nothing at all.

I think I inherited your storytelling, which is to say I am full of words and they are fighting to get out.

> And here is the wholest truth:
> maybe everyone has the capacity to learn,
> but I cannot be everyone's teacher.

Rule #40: It's ok to get fucked up sometimes, but seriously, you feel like shit the next day (not to mention your dreams).

    I have fallen asleep at night covered in salt: yours,
                                  mine, or the ocean's.
                                That sun turned skin.
                    That languid warm-limbed sprawl, as in
                        after a long run or our bodies, cleaved.

But my life is one perpetual sunrise.
I stretch my jaw at the yawn of dawn,
open my eyes to face the maw of high noon,
which chases me, eclipse-like, altogether too slow
to arrive and then over and past in the single moment
I am distracted from watching for it.
I wake up red, frosting the horizon a blood orange
that may be me if the wind is blowing right.
Some mornings, my clouds all shift to other horizons
and I am free to feel clean. Others, my storm paints
itself purple: the colors of war. I wake with
the taste of rust already in my mouth.
And still others, my fog lowers itself heavy,
rests itself tired on my clay. It blurs the edges
of the day and I walk through the hours with
 my eyes glazed, half open, hands outstretched
for someone else to lead or at least to warn of walls.

These are the gray days, when crumbs turn
to concrete dust and talcum, when my joints swell
so I cannot even imitate fists, when sleep is a
silver fish, slow, but just out of reach
in the murky water, waiting with bait and teeth
for me to drift off into its stagnant trap.

I fall into dreams without falling into sleep.
There is my mouth and your hands, and the feeling
of graveyard dirt at the roots of my hair where you
tried to yank me back into the living.
The prostitute in my soul is moaning and stirring
her embers. I could take just about anyone home
with me. There are things that I know
and one of them is this: the only thing I've ever
been good at is people, and the secret is this —
the better I get at people, the worse I get at myself.

Tonight, the boy at the bar has an Indiana drawl
and chiseled muscles and large knuckles
that are sure with a pool cue between them
and I'd like to be touched that surely, surely.
I like the taste of your teeth and the tingling heat
lines drawing themselves between our fluted parts
but you smell like a bedroom over a garage
in the summer and I've been trying to leave that
part of my story finished.

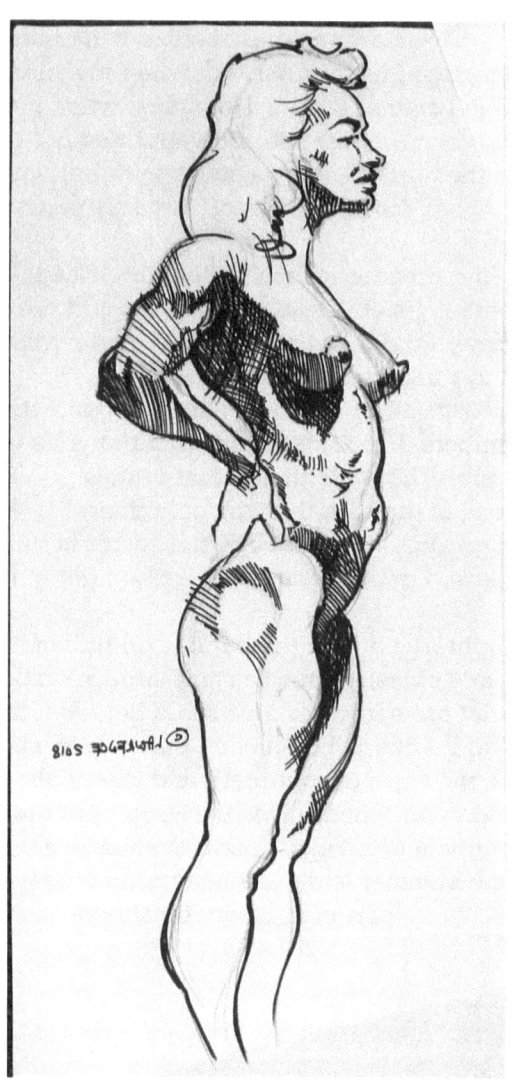

Rule #37: Make all your stories new stories.

> And the next day,
> I'm staring at the naked drawings
> of my best friend and I realize that none of them
> captured her bleeding and that means
> they will probably miss my sunflowers.

Since when is being untouchable a good thing?
I like to be touched.

> */Please / touch me/*

Maybe I escaped into books because my reality
was too heavy to speak, too dark to see,
too slippery to touch.

> I am still an eight-year-old girl sitting naked
> on the toilet trying not to think about
> the elephant in the room.

Rule #25: Don't sleep with anyone you don't want to smell like.

I have woken myself from sleep drenched in sweat:
    mine, yours, or the ocean's, that reoccurring
        open water nightmare of all of his hands.

I think there's something broken in me. Like how
kissing him was slippery, and brought back
a memory of old things, slipping, a piece I did not
need to know but now own all the same. How he
tasted — like you, and also you, ever so faintly —
and I think this might have been what I meant
when I said you're allergic: you all have the same
hands and do not ask permission to touch me
with them and you do not touch my bones with them.
Am I so twisted beyond repair that I feel danger
in everything safe, feel safe in the face of any danger?
Can I untangle this mess?
Can I get better?

    I'm selfish, but god forgive me, sometimes I think
        I can smell him on me; I knew how he'd taste
                before he ever touched me.

Remember when you drove yourself to court,
you looked at the lawyer and apologized,
all the while still tasting wine on the plastic cap

of your mug from months ago, broken bras and
bloody rags smashed in the snow of an anonymous
parking lot. You've washed your hands a thousand
times, cut your fingernails so short that his oil
can't still be under the ones growing there now
but it is, it is, and today you get to leave it here
in a puddle of whiskey you set on fire with
the traffic summons that's making you relive it now.

    I am still an eight-year-old girl sitting naked on
  the toilet, its edges digging into my shivering legs,
   trying not to think about the elephant in my head.

        I'm still learning how to forgive myself.

I wanted to ask you what you pray for when you pray,
but I didn't get the chance. I used to pray that
I could take on all the problems of the world,
have them ruin me and me alone because of how
many other people it'd save the heartbreak, and
I was ruined anyways — naïve, I know, because
I know now that some of the things I'm most
grateful for were the worst things to have happened —
twisted, I know. Anyways, it came true anyways,
because I carry things for people who have stories
to tell and things to get rid of, who need to breathe
a little easier. And I wouldn't have it any other way,
because I get to human real fast, to real real fast, but
I'm starting to realize now that I might get gratitude,
but no one wants to keep the girl who reminds them
of the things they told her, trying to forget.

Maybe the reason I want to be a surgeon is
because I will be able to freely speak the language
of trauma without talking about myself.

I think the thing that made me so disconnected,
the thing that removed me from living — that first,
that worst, that maybe-half-remembered catalyst —
might have also been the best thing, for giving me
a glimpse of what it feels like to be so far removed,
for giving me the ability to recognize a shadow
on someone else's face
and draw them back in.

Rule #17: Climb everything.

    When you are compelled to run fifteen miles
        in the drifts of winter, do not question it.
    Burn your lungs on the cold and spend the rest
        of the night trembling.

Listen to all your old music:
    The song that you played on repeat
to ward off the panic of Organic Chemistry.
    The one that you still hum in the shower.
    The one that colors your eyelids purple.
    The one that makes your feet twitch.
Let the chords deepen your bones, wrap a melody
around you like a scarf to ward off the chill.
When you're homesick, take these small bits
and feel them: like the smell of your mother's kitchen,
barefoot on the tile floor with the familiar sunlight
streaming through the back window past
all of the house plants.

        Confront your demons.
    Turn them human: when that's terrifying,
      turn them senses, turn them places.
          Go there.
          Smell them.
Call their taste to your tongue, feel their hands
        on your skin.

Scrub them off,
spit them out,
breathe in all the fresh air you can.
Do not let their ghosts make a home of you.

What if cancer is just the next evolutionary step?
And we keep killing our growth instead of seeing
which of us will survive it?

I've been programming my brain with a logic
that prays for the root of my problems rather than
the symptoms, which is to say: I am learning.

I keep sharing all these stories, yelling them
into the horizon, whispering them
through door cracks or the spaces between fingers
in the hopes that someone is listening
someone who will learn from them.
Maybe then they'll have been worth it.

Speaking in front of people requires no confidence,
only a flight of tongue and the ability to will down
your blush. I used to stoplight my cheeks
at any set of eyes, but I haven't gone red in years
and my tongue has a mind of its own.

Of course I can be silent.
I am silent.
A lot of the time.
Staring through the walls. Through you.
I'm listening. I've learned not to try to speak
when things are moving so fast that they are still.

And when I met you, I wanted to tell you
all of these things that have been piling themselves
in my throat for so long; for so long I have been
ears and eyes, lips retired to do nothing but kiss
or smile. It's my hands that speak for me now,
wandering lost on your skin, searching for some
friendly place to whisper my secrets where you will
not have to carry them. Because there are many ways
to speak of trauma: I am stoic, I am strong, I am angry,
I am sad or lost and some days even I am wailing
but when I tell this story it is still missing words:
like for his face, how the shadows traced it and
moved like he said they sometimes still did for him.
For how he tasted, like a forced forgotten memory,
half surfaced casket that I tried to bury under
concrete and tree roots until it poisoned
the whole damn forest growing in my head. For the
broken things, the painful lack of tear ducts, the
cinnamon whiskey fog that numbs the red that got
lost until the next weekend, a disassociated vision
in the melting snow. There are words for these things,
unspeakable words, and on the bad days they swim
up behind my eyes or rear their gargoyle spines
at dusk to chase me down the twisted
wooded paths that are left.

> Do you ever feel like you're moving too fast
> to connect to anything at all?
> Like you're moving through time
> instead of with it?

Rule #23: You don't always have to have a reason.

On days when I can still feel hands at my throat,
I look into the mirror and see what is swimming
in my eyes. I close them when I smile.

I've been running my whole life. My mom told me that,
when I was trying to explain how it clears my head,
        how I need it, how I'm sorry for how I act
        and what tumbles out of my mouth when
        I have to move. It makes sense, I guess:
the expression like sad, or inevitable, or knowing
                wrapped up in her face.

/I have an affinity for complicated emotions /
/Don't give me happy / or sad / give me angry-joy
and underwater caves to explore with only
a single matchstick leftover / as in every time
I've ever been split ax-open/

        Ever been so tired your hands stop working?
        That you wake up in the middle of the night
        to your whole body twitching and shaking,
        feeling out its own exhausted connections
        as if to remind itself it still has limbs?

But some nights you know that staying awake
is better than what's waiting for you if you sleep.
On days like those, I want to ask you:
do you know what it feels like to not be safe
in your head because someone went up there
and moved around all the furniture
and now it leaves bruises on your shins
when the lights are off?

                              I want to ask you:
                     do you remember what it feels like
   to be scrubbing someone else's scent off your skin
              for weeks, and a taste in your mouth
                  that even vodka won't sterilize?
                          I want to ask you:
             can you listen? Just for a minute?
Because there are things that I want to tell you that
I do not want you to hear. Can you cover your ears
  and hold my hand while I cough up these shards
    of glass? I promise I'll clean up the mess later.
        I've been practicing that my entire life.

   You are still an eight-year-old girl sitting naked
            on the toilet, trying not to think
                about anything at all.

I'm realizing now that realizing anything
about yourself is a good thing — and I'm realizing
that the reason I'm so awkward the morning after
is probably the combination of a lot of things,
and I started to shut down again. And now

whenever I have sex with someone new
it flashes back to that, like pot-fueled-paranoia
or sets of hands that cannot contain their tempers,
or that fucking traffic court. It's also probably why
I get nervous opening up, knowing that people
exist who would take all that I am
and turn me against myself, that the potential
is always there but more so the fact of it is there.
And one day I'll tell someone that story,
the whole story, but now I'll also be able to tell
them about today, and how I learned a little bit
more about myself, and started practicing letting
go and just being.

        And then, on the days after these days,
I remember: that this is what **Time** does. It gives
you more things to remember. And things are
never good, nor bad, things always and only just are.
And this is the price that is paid, the burden borne,
        the gift granted, the present unwrapped
for a person who is lives the very most of a life
        in the amount of **Time** given to them.

I am sleepless next to you and your brain is loud
and I cannot force my joints to unhinge.
You are sleepless next to me and the echo
chamber of our pantomimed sleep breathing coats
the skin between us in sweat. My brain is a cave
and all your unheard thoughts are shooting off
cannonfire into the spaces I've cleared there for
someone to inhabit. I am sleepless next to you

and I hope my unsoft edges on yours are nice,
at least for now, at least for tonight. My joints
will not unhinge; you have me unhinged. I cannot
sleep because you, too, are awake and the tension
between us is a sheen of salt water skin dripping
into an underground cavern somewhere where we
both could speak out loud and feel how our echoes
overlap, like tides. We are not sleeping but I am
dreaming, here, wrapped up in the hinge of your arms
that is keeping me unmoving and unsteady, dreaming
of the spaces in your brain that pantomime dreams,
the ones that move a little bit like me, the ones
that look a little bit like this: us, unmoving,
pretending to sleep, to dream, of unhinging
each other to let in the tide.

/An argument against cynicism, / or /
You Are Too Smart to Already Be Done Learning/

/There is a traffic sign in my head that reads /
The World Is Broken */ It glows a poisonous orange
that makes the dark corners up there
swallow themselves whole and still come up empty/*

*/In the emptiness, the reverberating echo
quadruples into a metronome as bland as gray /
It whispers /* ***Life Is Meaningless*** */
and coats the whole room in cigarette ash /
TV static/ and damp couch crumbs/*

/There is a ghost who sometimes sleeps
in my bed / He appears on the bad nights
as the hands and breath of every person
who has ever used their skin as sandpaper
on my edges / and I curl up on the corner closest
to the window / desperate for fresh air / clean skin /
and drift off into a sleep that hums like
a neon diner sign / **Love Is a Dead Language**/

/In the mourning / waking up with a matchstick
for a tongue / ready to conquer myself
only to set me burning back to ash all over again /
I am often struck by the realization / that /
This Is All There Is/

/I've been reaching all these conclusions
and each one is a bass drum deep in my chest/

/You can look at the world and say /
the world is horrible / it is evil / it is full of war
and hate and hunger and meaningless violence
and pollution / But that means you've given up /
And you may as well be dead at that point because
you will have died long before you're actually gone/

/You can look at the world and say / the world
is beautiful / it is full of joy and laughter and
wonderful nice smelling things /
And if your world is / then you are lucky /
but there is more to the world than
just your world / and if you don't realize that
 you'll be deluding yourself/

*/Or you can look at the world and say /
this world is beautiful / It is ugly / It is full
and it is empty / and there are parts that you may not
want to see but you feel them there all the same /
And you will look at the world and say /
this world is not perfect / But it has potential /
it is the world / and I can help to shape it /
And that / to me / is the only life worth living/*

*/And if you accept this / you will never be a peaceful
person again / You will live in constant paradox /
but if you can accept your contradictions
it will not matter / because you will be alive /
and the truest alive that I know how to be/*

*/This is understanding / of the world / of myself /
of you / in the most honest way I know/*

Rule #29: Listen more than you tell.

It would be the simplest thing in the world,
to just appreciate all that we are, to stop this
mindless competition. Of course we are not
the same. There will be places where I shine
and others that belong to you
and we can invite each other there
and have picnics.
I would like that, I think.
I think that would be nice.

> I don't expect you to understand.
> That's not the point.

All I'm looking for is someone to listen.
Someone who wants to.
Someone who wants to know me,
who wants to share right back.
I could do that for you, too, you know.

>All I want is someone to keep me grounded,
>who can break into this spiral because they know
>right where I am, and drag me back to here,
>to now. It wouldn't be hard. I promise.
>You could do it. This is me, spelling it out for you,
>telling you you could, showing you how.

**Rule #45: Touch everyone.
It makes you happy.**

I think I just miss being able to love someone.
It's a privilege, really, because for some reason
it's taboo to love recklessly, to love carefree,
to love anyone and everyone you cross paths with.
But it's also the thing everyone's looking for,
the thing everyone's trying to fill,
the most important thing.
And I had but a poor imitation but god
it doesn't take much to get you hooked, does it?

> I want to introduce myself to everyone I meet.
> *Hello. Are you my person?*
> And wouldn't that save us a hell of a lot of time?

I want someone who I can run wild with.
Someone who is reverent under any phase
of the moon ... who is not afraid of heat or cold
or heights, who calls upon god or allah or peter pan
to ignite the spark in them that compels them
to climb mountains or electrical poles,
or spring marathons into the dusk on winged soles,
or scream into windstorms and let our hair crust
with salt, naked in the burning ocean sunlight.
Baby ... life is a grand adventure and I'm as exciting
as they come. Whatever it throws at us, I promise,

I'm game. And I could do it alone.
I don't need anyone for anything, not really.
But I'm in the market for a partner in crime.

    How do I tell you that you make me feel like
operating rooms, all alien-familiar, exciting thrill
       of being home? I don't, of course I don't.
And we're not going to ramble, unfortunately,
I already gave you some of that and I think it got
    under your skin. But good. I won't apologize.
    I am looking for something deeper than skin,
and just because I happen to want to taste yours
         doesn't mean I don't want to tangle
         your brainwaves even more.

       I never liked Aphrodite
    but I still find myself searching
for lingering gazes in crowded rooms.

And this is the elegance of the prostitute:
she smiles at every face she passes by.

         Hello. I am here.
    Please see me. Please be happy to see me.

    This, too, is a kind of touching.

I'm looking for something a little more cerebral, but
with skin. Because this is how I communicate best:
with my mouth. And baby, I'd love to show you
what I can do with my tongue,

how deep my throat goes, how my voice drops
an octave when I'm occupied.

    I am more than just a girl, and I've been wrong
      before but you seem to be more than just a boy.
But let's meet on common ground. We seem to have
enough of that to build a bedframe worth breaking.
I extinguish matches with my saliva: I could ash
         you into poetry with a tongue like that.

        I think you need an adventure,
          one with a wild laugh.
         (But first I need to know:
        Are you afraid of heights?)

/Let's bridge the gap / Connect our dissonance/
Let's stroll soberdrunk through the streets
of the world touching skins / Your warmth
and mine / mixing / melting the snow that's raining
down on our collective mushroom cloud mind /
hovering overhead like a cloud sewn out of sunshine /
We can get as high as the oil painted mountains
in the distance at this altitude / bottle up the feeling
of the world turning beneath us / and savor our tipping /
We could exist in this haze as just our fingertips /
blindly feel the ways our whorls line up / We don't
need anything but this / the smell of pine smoke and
hot water steam / of cold sweat / and my frozen
hair tips tracing snowflakes on your chest. /
And both of us dripping with morning dew/

I've come to the conclusion that there isn't enough
purple in the world: look around. Once you notice
it's hard not to. And maybe that's why I've always
been attracted to blue — we could violet a sunset
of the deepest orchid. They've all been the wrong
shade so far, a little too slippery, psychedelic, unreal.

But something about yours smells like greenhouses
and sugarcane jungles and I'd love to explore
your tiled eyes a little deeper.

*/Your skin smells like merlot / all purple sugar /
and your hair is a newborn deer / I wobble
at the knock-knees with my hand tangled up
in your head/ Freight train hands / you taste hard /
like autumn cider or unsmooth marble warmed
under the august sun / Kiss me again /
I dare you/*

There are the movers and shakers and doers
of the world, the ones who generate the current
and then there are the ones who remember to look
up, who find purple, who remind us of the beauty
of the flow and I do not understand why
it is so hard to believe that I could be both.

I was thinking about navigating geography:
how being in a car on an unfamiliar road\
sends me spiraling into panic, but I regularly try
to get myself lost in the woods and never worry
about finding my way out because I tell direction

by water or a black bird migration, and somewhere
in here is a metaphor for a life path that is only
my own, to leave behind the asphalt expectations
of the world and break free of all this goddamned
traffic. Something about cavorting through tree
shadow in nothing but skin, weaving holes through
the brush to the heart of the woods…

When I think about love, real love, I still think about
gold people, and there are few I've ever met.
There is a lot of me and all of it is on fire, but I still
think I could be good to someone, one day.
There are things I'd like to show them, to teach
them, like love and touching, and how warm
it's possible to be, how heat is exponential,
like hearts, when you're not burning alone.
And I'm not a patient person but dammit,
for a feeling like that I'd play the long game.

The first time you tell a story out loud
is a powerful thing. It loses a bit of heat every time
it's told and there are stories that I will scream
until they are smaller than the pieces that they
broke me into; others, I'm saving for someone who
might see their special.

I am old enough to know that I am not in love with you,
and wise enough to know that I very well could be
one day. I don't know how to tell you that I think we
inhabit the same spaces, at different times, that if I
got to know you better maybe we could explode
our dimensions together – I don't know if I have to.

And I'm finding all these words for all these things —
　　　　like how you bring out my warm and
　　　the catch in my throat when we locked eyes
　　on top of me — I did not exist in my body then
but I do now and god I'd love to pin you down for
　　　　　　a minute to do things to you with it.
　　　　　　You, with your bonfire summer musk.
　　　I could drink you in without a single worry
as to what all the smoke is doing to my lungs.

And I love your human, but if I show you mine
　　　you'll probably just get bored of me.

Rule #31: There will be very few people who get you, and none of them who get all of you, and that's fine because you're fun anyways.

There are five muscles in your body that are optional.
                      Some people simply don't have them.
              Does that mean you're more or less evolved?
Do you think a lion born in captivity ever dreams
                 of hotter sands, if it feels out of place
                    like a person born in the wrong time?

I would wear out all my shoes if it meant
I knew how to stand with you in yours,
even for only a minute. That's the whole point,
isn't it? That in spite of anything we've ever had to
deal with, get over, move on from, we're here now
having this conversation. That's all we are, different
combinations of the same version of struggle. So we
lie down together on roofs in the dark, in unfamiliar
beds, smelling like liquor or tobacco or skunk, trying
to jigsaw our broken bits to see where we fit together.

   And now I spill my secrets to strangers, knowing
      full well you might as well be one of them.

Have you ever felt completely alone among family
and neighbors who grew old as you grew up,
from diapers to now, but somewhere along the
way it feels like you never were taught how to
connect, and now you're stuck inside listening to
the fireworks laughing outside and the hole in your
chest expands but you know it'll only be worse to
go outside and watch them stare at it through you.

> There is a language that everyone knows and
> it feels like belonging but I missed that day in
> kindergarten.

Have you ever felt too old to be this young?

And then there are the days when people tell you
what you mean to them, what you said to change
them, what you did to shape them, and you go
about the rest of it with that echo in your chest
that says: *I matter, I matter.*

> We're at a black-tie concert, and my mom
> drunkenly tells me that she knew from the moment
> I was born that I wasn't hers, that I'm supposed to
> do something bigger, like Joan of Arc, and I guess
> I'm not crazy for being drawn to the teenage girl
> who was burned alive, for never feeling like I fit.
> I tell her I didn't mind, that I know, that I carry her
> name with me for a reason. I hope whatever it is
> I have to do that it doesn't hurt her. She's stronger
> than she lets herself be sometimes, and always

for other people, and that's the truest way of loving
that I know.

And then the music started and my hands went
warm and I practiced pulling colors out of the air.
Itzak Pearlman is a paraplegic cinemaphile, and all
romance. He played the Robin Hood and Marion
love song, and I tried to cry, but couldn't so instead
we screamed ACDC all the way home, and it was
still yearning, still wanting, still a little lonely, but it
was also good.

> Full orchestra symphonies sound like running
> barefoot tribal through a burning wood; if you're
> swaying with the bodies conducted in the tide you
> get to be the drums.

I am a heat source, passion sink. I was born a little
closer to the tap than most so maybe that's why
I can umbilical myself to the root of other people's
patterns so easily. And true passion is very rarely
a healthy thing. In fact, it demands that we forgo
health, forgo connection, give up well roundedness
and bigger picture thinking for this immediacy.
And if my passion is for all of these things that
it intrinsically denies me, it is not some great
mystery as to why I'm burning.

> Freud limited his definition of libido to just sex.
> A lust for life deserves an unadulterated name,
> a word that tumbles off tongues to fill all the
> tumblers instead of the other way around.

If god speaks in tongues and all we mortals can
hope to pronounce is poetry, isn't that our version:
universally understood metaphor without rules:
or music, where the color of the sound you make
is more important than what you say, or art at
all, where you feel what you mean. And isn't
that what tongues would sound like, like Monet
painting the Hallelujah chorus under church bells
and a sound so high it stands all your skin
at attention, so low it melts your bones?

Ever wonder why people bow their heads to pray?
It's involuntary if you do it right.

Imagine every language ever invented, all being
spoken at the same time: the most human noise
chaotically possible, spreading like warm wax.
That's as close to god as we'll ever be able
to speak.

What does it mean when you paint with the colors
that make you feel angry-alive? When you're the
one writing the words that move you?
Where is the source?
It cannot only be you, surely.

The inside of the church smells like a ski shop:
warm wax and metal edges and something pine.
And I am in moss green, surrounded by all this
guilt and feeling Mediterranean.

    The answer to the question that's strangling itself
        on the back of your tongue is this:
     Get comfortable with being uncomfortable.
          Embrace the chaos.
     Come to terms with your contradictions.
        You should know this by now...
       haven't you been listening at all?

The inside of the church smells like a ski shop:
warm wax and metal edges and something pine
and burning. And I am in moss green, surrounded
by all this guilt and feeling vaguely like an olive,
saturated in my salt.

  I think you need to hear this and I don't know why
            but please listen, really listen:
                 You can't let them win.
      The voices, of everyone who ever made you
        feel worthless, made you feel less than,
          the hands that tried to bleed you out,
           the teeth that tried to eat you alive.
     Even if it's your own voice, your own hands
  you have to fight, tooth and nail to find happy.

Because I had come to terms with the inevitability
of my own death a long time ago, sitting at my desk
holding a bottle of pills in one hand, a pen in the
other, your name dripping in ink off my tongue.

*/Someone once said that human beings
are destined to radiate or drain / and we all know
which one you are / And here I was / lending you
my sunflowers/*

GIRL just be yourself.
Shine, baby. Shimmer shimmy your way into
legend and song ... you know you're capable of
being every boy's wet-dream one night stand.
You know you've got what it takes to deepen
the bass, to start up a rhythm that leaves O-faces
on everyone in the audience.
Embrace the world and show it a good time.
You want to be a fucking legend?
BE A FUCKING LEGAND.
Don't let anyone hold you back, hold you down,
keep you waiting.
You want to shake shit up and make shit happen?
You want to leave impressions like firework trails
and memories that bring the spark back
into aged eyes?
Make it happen.
And if that makes you feel a little untouchable?
Good.

The inside of the church smells like something
pine is burning and I am crackling under it, too.
And I am green, but all this guilt killed off the
moss.

I think that it's important to earn your happiness.
But that's only half of it: in order to truly be happy,
you have to be grateful for it.
>   Where you came from.
>   What you've been.
>   Who you are now.
>   The direction you're heading.

You have to accept all of it, not to carry it, but to be
free of it, to be grateful for it, be thankful for it.
All of it.

> Remember that time you realized you had
> something to lose? You have emptied yourself,
> retraced your roots to primal, to angry joy,
> to burned matchtips, rekindled your bonfire heart.
> And you have something to lose now,
> of course you do.
> Because you have something to offer.

I've been erasing forgive me from all my poetry.

If all we are is our history, then consider this my
Renaissance. I am in full bloom, every branch of me
turned ivy curious and the ferns here are Jurassic.
And I love you, but if the colors are too intense
please leave.

> I just wanna DO something, ya know?
> Something meaningful. Something significant.
> Even if it doesn't seem important, every fiber
> of my body is singing *put me to work,*
> *put me to use, let me be useful, I want to help.*

She tells me:

> *I think you were chained up and then set to fly
> all at once and your body hasn't gotten a chance
> to settle yet. But be unapologetically you, because
> that you has nearly burned herself down
> with the world over and over and at the same
> time is everything and everywhere and powerful
> and brave and beautiful and bright and genuinely
> passionate. I feel like you're finding a way to fill
> the world around you without questioning yourself.
> It's not even a stupid crushes thing. I think you sell
> yourself short, calling it that. You recognize things
> that are significant and that isn't stupid at all.*

Maybe that's why I can't sleep: all this pent-up
potential. You corked me for too long and thank
god I exploded when I did. In physics and logic
and topography and neural networks, things
tend towards their most local lowest potential.
But I've tunneled through that shit to find a new
equilibrium and let me tell you it's liberating.

                Maybe that's why my brain is singing
this siren song: now I have something to lose.

I exist in a different time zone. Cross into my
dimension: the days here are long, the moments
endless, the minutes between moments are
underwater breath lengths, desperately kicking for

a surface that shimmers an infinite blue
out of grasp.
And full.
  My days are full.
This life is full, I am full, as full as that salt blue
horizon.

 Maybe manic pixie dream girls are like fairies:
 if you don't believe in them anymore, when you
 grow out of them, they die to make room for reality.

             And once again the world
              has gotten too small for me.
     College has started to feel like high school again
             and I'm not sure how I feel about it.
                    Not great, probably.
             But I'm brushing the edges of the box
            with my wings, poking out breath holes
     with the talons I've grown in the last four years,
              sharpening the edges of my feathers
                       and my shinbones.
                The real world is a cruel place,
                         so I've heard.
                         I'll be ready.

**Rule #38: Fall in love
with your friends and your life
and the world.**

> Today I can feel myself being extra contagious,
> so I search for eyes to smile at.
> It's so pretty outside today ...
> it's snowing all fluffy.

When did everyone get so anxious?
I was raised not to care what other people thought,
only to care about what my own effect was.
Everyone's just looking for someone to give a shit:
I am not excluded from this, of all things.
But I also know that I can care, and therefore
I should, of course, anything to take some of the
burden. I was born with this urge, and it's a skill
I've since been practicing.

> */A little bit of fresh air to cut the stagnant stale /
> One curt tongue / thank god for people
> who take the leap / to speak and mind / have they
> all been thankful for me, too/*

You could describe my confidence today as
obnoxious, or as having something to do with why
everyone always thinks I'm a lesbian.

There is no time for side projects
when you're playing the long game.
And in spite of my innate impatience,
Mea Culpa, this fire I was born with,
I have always saved a few embers off to the side,
just for this.
There are things worth waiting for
one of them
is you.

Rule #48: Don't settle for something that's attainable if it's not really what you want.

>   There are moments in your life
>   that are completely surreal.

>   Do you ever feel like an island?
> Like you're stranded and surrounded by gurgling blue
>   but there's lots of sunshine and coconuts
>   so really what's there to complain about?

There are days when you spin for the world,
spin and are dizzy to the point of vomiting
or passing out or going gray or seeing red,
and then there are days when the world
spins for you, and you can feel it all around you,
every constellation, every connection. You can feel
the spin and you are still in the center of it all
and it feels so good have gravity.

>   You ever felt your own warmth and fall in love?
>   You ever romanticize yourself and realize
>   you don't need anyone else for that?

And this is the aftermath: you finally get to where
you were trying to go and you look around at
who's left with you as the dust clears and it seems

that suddenly the faces surrounding you are all
strange and new.

   I ran into you today and I realized from the smile
on my face and my contagious heat you probably
thought I was in love but I am not. I am merely
moonstruck with my own life and I wouldn't have it
any other way because I did this, and no one else.
And no one can take this from me now.

Don't mistake this for natural: this is earned
happiness, the truest kind I know.

I'm embracing my manic pixie dream girls.
You wish we'd fuck you,
but we've got shit to do.

Rule #43: Be a badass bitch but also love everyone.

Maybe we'll look back one day and wonder
why we ever took ourselves so seriously.
But if we're together while we're laughing,
then who's to say it wasn't worth it?

> You know that shade of purple?
> The dusty one?

I'm cracking off my crust, peeling apart my layers,
shedding every soiled skin I have ever been,
burning myself clean with this joy,
this effervescent soap-bubble-laughter
that is gurgling out of my chest
in a sunflower sunshine waterfall.

> You ever spend a whole day smiling
> without knowing why?

/Give me your sobbing laughter /
your most radiant sorrow /
Give me your weight finally set down behind you /
give me the dust of your splintering shackles /
every unshed tear / every unshone smile /
This is the truest joy I know /
Bottle this feeling /

Bottle it / just a sliver / and savor it / save it / share/

You remember that night?
Yea, me too.

And to think I almost gave this up for you.
To think it was even a thought.
You are not worth this joy;
this is not something you could have ever understood.
This supersedes the idea of love and sex and skin
and the smell of your spit
and anything you could have offered
would have been nothing but matchstick fire:
temporary compared to this inferno joy.
Thank god.
And if there is a love, a true love, a real love,
I imagine that's the only thing that could rival this.

You know that painting?
you know: the one that makes you feel big
and small and angry-alive all at once?

/I am everything that is featherlight and fire /
Is this what flying feels like/

I have only felt this feeling a few times in my life,
and never this powerfully. This feeling that
I am here, I've arrived. That I'm where and when
I'm supposed to be.

>   You know that song?
>   You know, the one that's not really musical
>   or even lyrical, but every time you listen to it
>   you feel a thing so specific that you show it to all
>   your friends and lovers to see which ones really
>   get it.

I am about to spend my life saving others.
This is what I've been waiting forever for.
I can't possibly be damaged goods.
I can't possibly be ruined: I have too much to offer.
And I've earned this happiness.
Finally, I deserve it.

>   You ever imagine a future thing
>   like you're living in it now?
>   You ever try to paint with words?
>   Do you remember what you painted?
>   How it tasted?
>   Did you save it somewhere, in that box
>   in your closet with all the letters and pictures?
>   You ever still take it down?

We keep telling ourselves we're going to be done
one day but I think we all know deep down
we'll never be done.

> This is why I'm here. This is why I'm still alive.
> And every fiber of my heart muscle is singing it,
> every inch of my electric skin, every budding of

my tongue, every edge of my nails and teeth,
every dancing joint chopping at the acceleration
to pick up the pace. And I get to do this now.
I get to do this thing and I can't stop crying
and laughing and I don't know why but thank you,
thank you,
thank you.

Hello, world, I have arrived.

I cannot wait for the rest of my life.

And it's all going to be ok.

Because I get to end my story with this now,
this joy.

Rule #33: When in doubt, be a pirate.

        I'm embracing my manic pixie dream girls.
                You want to fuck us,
              but we're kind of busy.

There is a woman inside of me
who is constantly screaming.
She is the wind howling over the outstretched
neck of a green glass bottle, stirring her own
circular currents with humid sticky lungs.

            Look for the naked silhouette weaving
              between tree shadows at dusk,
           sparking the sulfur tips off matches
                to draw in the fireflies.
                  Of course that's me.

There is a woman in inside of me who is silent;
her lips were plastered into a grin long ago,
lock jawed grimace dripping, melting like wax.
There is no noise in her but a heartbeat.
And what a heartbeat it is.

        We all already have such a short time here:
              why are we fighting?

She moves through the places she feels comfortable
like a dancer: assured. Her bedroom, a wooded trail,
high-speed hospital hallway traffic, a weight room,
the barefoot backyard she grew from,
any body of water, any body, any body's story,
drunken party nights, textbook library days.
She blends into the background,
so natural she becomes part of the scene
and is therefore lost in it.

    Look for the girl who's dancing alone in the library.
                                        Of course that's me.

      You MUST to be excited about things.
    If you're not excited what's the fucking point?

    Look for the girl practicing ballet in hiking boots
                       in the middle of a Home Depot.
                                   Of course that's me.

There is a 20-year-old girl with gang signs
tattooed across her knuckles,
clutching the sides of the gurney
as we pull out her stitches.
She has a rod in her leg where it was shattered
by a stray bullet:
this, too, is me.

*/Give me the complicated / the bittersweet nostalgic
          unrequiescence / I want to nurse something /
              turn it over in my mouth like a marble /*

*with a different flavor on every corner / some new
expression of what it means to live and be human
on every face/*

Bring something different — something you —
into everything you do. Make it yours.

    Look for the girl barefooted and bloody-blistered
on the school bus home,
curled up next to the window
with a book in her head
covered in her own salt.
Of course that's me.

There was an 88-year-old woman at clinic
bragging about her Barbados tan lines
to the PA checking her hip replacement scar
and I am this too.

*/I love the way the word Grenada tastes
in my mouth / and one time I wrote a tribute
to the goddess / Barbadosa / while I sunned myself
on the island they named after her highway
car-wreck curves/*

    Time is a flat circle.

Let yourself drift.

Rule #1: There are no concrete rules to guide a life well lived.

                        And now, find me that horizon.

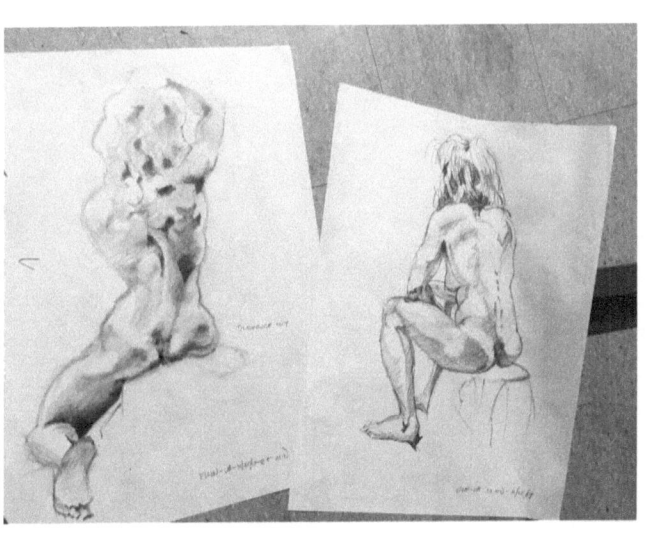

www.ingramcontent.com/pod-product-compliance
Lightning Source LLC
Chambersburg PA
CBHW030453010526
44118CB00011B/924